SOUL TIES

D0932381

THE FRANK HAMMOND BOOKLET SERIES

FRANK HAMMOND

SOUL TIES

by Frank Hammond

ISBN 10: 0-89228-016-6
ISBN 13: 978-089228-016-2

IMPACT CHRISTIAN BOOKS, INC.
332 Leffingwell Ave., Suite 101
Kirkwood, MO 63122
(314) 822-3309

www.impactchristianbooks.com

All passages are from the **NEW KING JAMES BIBLE** unless otherwise noted.

SOUL TIES

There are times when we experience spiritual truth before we understand it. I am reminded of an occasion when a group of ladies invited me to teach them about the baptism in the Holy Spirit. In the midst of the lesson, one of the ladies interrupted me to ask, "Can't you go ahead and pray for us to receive the baptism in the Holy Spirit and explain it to us later?" Because it was scriptural, that is what I did. Remember the one hundred and twenty who were baptized in the Holy Spirit on the day of Pentecost? They had the experience before they understood it.

My wife and I dealt with soul ties, through the ministry of deliverance, long before we had much understanding of them. In fact, long before someone introduced the designation "soul ties," we referred to them as "unholy alliances" or "perverse relationships." Through deliverance ministry, we encounter soul ties regularly and break their power over individuals' lives. Yes, soul ties are real, but what are they? What is the scriptural basis for understanding soul ties? How are they formed? Are they always demonic? What danger is there in soul ties? How can they be broken?

Good Soul Ties

Soul ties are formed when two or more people become bonded together. Some soul ties are good, and others are evil; some are holy, and some are ungodly. Our Holy God has ordained and sanctioned the soul ties of bonding between children and parents, husbands and wives, friends with friends and Christians with one another as members of the Body of Christ. Good soul ties are founded upon the law of love, which the Bible calls the law of Christ" (Gal. 6:2), and the "royal law" (Jas. 2:8). Thus, the soul ties approved by God represent the bonding of people together in agape love.

Ties of Marriage

In marriage, God purposes that a man and a woman "be joined... and the two shall become one flesh" (Eph. 5:31). They are to be bonded by love. "So husbands ought to love their own wives..." (Eph. 5:28). Within marriage, sexual union is an expression of God-approved love. The Bible declares that in marriage God joins a husband and wife, and let not man, through divorce, put asunder what God has joined together (see Matt. 19:6). Thus, divorce violently rends soul ties which God created. This tearing is what causes such pain, sorrow and trauma in divorce.

Ties of Friendship

"The soul of Jonathan was knit to the soul of David, and Jonathan loved him as his own soul" (1 Sam. 18:1). Here is another type of soul tie that is pure and based upon love. Jonathan loved David even to the laying down of his rights to the throne of Israel. "There is a friend who sticks closer than a brother" (Prov. 18:24). The Hebrew word for "friend" is rea, meaning "companion or lover." Oh, what a Friend we have in Jesus! For, "A friend loves at all times" (Prov. 17:17). Pure and holy soul ties are always based on godly love.

Parent/Child Soul Ties

Concerning Jacob's relationship with his son, Benjamin, we read, "His father loves him... His life is bound up in the lad's life, and his soul knit with the lad's soul" (Gen. 44:2, 30 AMPLIFIED BIBLE). Although Jacob's love for Benjamin was intensified because he believed his son, Joseph, had been killed; it illustrates the soul tie that exists between a parent and child.

When a child is born, the infant should be bonded to his parents. The parents convey their love to the child in many ways. When a healthy soul tie is formed, it ministers, throughout life, love and security to that child. The soul tie between parent and child stabilizes a child's personality.

Soul Ties Between Christians

The Church is made up of many members who are knit together and built up together through love. "The whole body joined and knit together by what every joint supplies... causes growth of the body for the edifying of itself in love" (Eph. 4:16, EMPHASIS MINE). The relationship between Christians in the Body of Christ is compared to the relationship of the various parts of the human body. The soul ties formed between members of the Body of Christ are not only desirable but necessary, for they enable the Body of Christ to mature and fulfill its calling.

DEMONIC SOUL TIES

Demonic soul ties are perversions of the good and holy. Good soul ties are founded upon love; demonic soul ties are founded upon lust. Remember that Satan cannot go beyond his limited rights: He must work within the framework of what he is allowed. When he gets the opportunity, he will pervert that which is pure.

Ties Formed Through Fornication

"Do you not know that he who is joined to a harlot is one body with her? For 'The two,' He says, 'shall become one flesh" (1 Cor. 6:16). Through sexual relationships outside of marriage, demonic soul ties are forged. Those who engage in sex outside of marriage, become the one flesh which God purposed solely for a husband and wife. Through adultery, an evil soul tie is created in lust, and this demonic soul tie destroys the holy union that is based upon mutual love and trust. When love and trust are betrayed through adultery, it is very difficult (although not impossible) to restore the shattered bonds of marital oneness.

Through physical attraction and passionate forms of affection outside of marriage, passions are aroused and demonic soul ties are created. The world's standard for couples is: dating, petting and marriage. God's order is: marriage, dating and petting. Excessive physical touching outside of marriage leads to the formation of a soul tie, and the lust that accompanies it makes the tie unclean, which opens the door for unclean spirits.

Perverse soul ties are not limited to those formed between persons of the opposite sex; they are also formed between those of the same sex through sodomy. Homosexuals, both gays and lesbians, attempt

6

to remove the stigma of their sin by referring to themselves as "lovers," but the Word of God declares that their motivation is lust: "Even their women changed the natural use for what is against nature: Likewise also the men, leaving the natural use of the woman, burned in their lust for one another" (Rom. 1:26–27, EMPHASIS MINE).

Furthermore, perverse soul ties include those formed between men and animals. Animals have souls (minds, emotions and wills); therefore, men can form soul ties with animals. The ultimate expression of sexual perversion is bestiality: lying carnally with animals. Some soul ties with animals fall short of bestiality and are characterized by false compassion and inordinate affection for animals.

When Adam needed a companion with whom he could become one flesh, every animal in all creation passed in review before him, and "Adam gave names to all the livestock, and to the birds of the air, and to every [wild] beast of the field; but for Adam there was not found a helper meet (suitable, adapted, complementary) for him" (Gen 2:20, AMP). A soul tie with an animal is a perversion.

Ties with Evil Companions

"Do not be so deceived and misled! Evil companionships (communion, associations) corrupt and deprave good manners and morals and character."

1 Cor. 15:33, AMP

One is readily influenced by his friends, so it is important to choose righteous and holy friends.

Soul ties with evil companions will ensnare you, and you will find yourself entangled in wickedness.

"Thorns and snares are in the way of the perverse; He who guards his soul will be far from them... Make no friendship with an angry man... lest you learn his ways and set a snare for your soul."

Prov. 22:5, 24–25 (emphasis mine)

Perverted Family Tie

Within a family, there are close soul ties, any of which Satan is eager to pervert. The soul tie between parent and child can be healthy and beneficial, except when it continues into the adult life of the child. The familiar expression, "cutting the apron strings," actually speaks of severing the soul tie between the parent and an adult offspring, When a son or daughter is ready for marriage, the soul tie with the parents must be terminated in order for the soul tie between husband and wife to be formed. Therefore, God decrees,

"A man shall leave his father and mother and be joined to his wife..."

Eph. 5:31

When the father gives his daughter in marriage, he severs the soul tie with her in consideration of her husband. When the filial soul tie is not severed at the proper time, then that which was good and beneficial becomes evil through control and possessiveness.

For one to "leave his father and mother" is not to be understood as breaking relationships with parents. Rather, it speaks of a maturing of the parent/child relationship that accompanies the maturing of the son or daughter. One must never stop honoring his Father and mother for this is a commandment with promise (Exod. 20:12).

Sexual perverseness within family relationships has become alarmingly prevalent. This perversion occurs when there is an incestuous copulation between father and daughter, mother and son, brother and sister, father-in-law and daughter-in-law, mother-in-law and son-in-law, or other close family ties.

When the essential bonding between parents and child is missed at birth, the child is left with a sense of incompleteness that can leave him restless and searching for love-bonding throughout life. This is the reason that so many who did not bond with their parents in love are targets for Satan's use.

A pastor and his wife had five children of their own plus an adopted daughter. The six children were raised with impartial love, spiritual influences and training. Why, then, was this adopted daughter the only child who was drawn into the world and its rebellion? It was that this particular child was abandoned and rejected by her own flesh-and-blood parents. In spite of the love offered by the adoptive parents, the spirit of rejection kept her from accepting that love. In her quest for love-fulfillment, she became wed to the world in lust.

Soul Ties with the Dead

When a family member or close friend dies, the soul tie formed with that person must be dissolved. The period of sorrow, following the death of a loved one, is a time of adjustment during which the soul tie is ended, yet the fond and loving memories remain.

Bible examples of mourning for the dead teach us that days of mourning should be limited. Mourning normally lasted from seven to thirty days. When Jacob died, Joseph "observed seven days of mourning for his father" (Gen. 50:10). "Now when the congregation saw that Aaron was dead, all the house of Israel mourned for Aaron thirty days" (Num. 20:29). "And the children of Israel wept for Moses... thirty days. So the days of weeping and mourning for Moses ended" (Deut. 34:8).

Prolonged mourning may indicate the continuation of the soul tie, and the stress of extended grief will create an opportunity for spirits of sorrow, grief and loneliness to enter. Also, if one attempts to communicate with the deceased loved one, he can easily acquire a familiar spirit.[1]

A woman who came to us for deliverance had never formed satisfactory soul ties with her three children. She was afraid to form the needed ties, and there was a reason for this reluctance. She was also very possessive of her grandchildren. Furthermore, when she realized that she was nearing the time of menopause, she became obsessed with the desire to have another child. When she heard a teaching on soul ties, she realized her problem and came for ministry.

The Lord showed her that she had never broken the soul ties with three babies she had miscarried and one that was stillborn. Normal soul ties had been formed while these babies were in her womb. The loss of these children, which occurred prior to the birth of her other children, made her afraid to bond (form soul ties) with her living children, lest she also lose them. Within herself she had never ceased sorrowing over the infants lost through miscarriage and stillbirth. Thus, she was never really satisfied with the children she raised. She tried to fill the emptiness within by bonding with her grandchildren. She was released from bondage when she realized her reason for wanting another child.

---

1 *Confronting Familiar Spirits* by Frank Hammond, available at
   www.impactchristianbooks.com

Demonic Soul Ties within the Church

Sometimes there are factions within the Body of Christ that oppose the Body unity sung about in the familiar hymn, "Blest be the tie that binds our hearts in Christian love." There are evil soul ties represented by cliques that cause division in the Body. Such groups oppose Church unity and the blending of the Body together.

> But God composed the body, having given greater honor to the part that lacks it, that there should be no schism in the body, but that the members should have the same care for one another.
>
> 1 Cor. 12:24, 25

Cliques work against the mutual care that Christ designed for His Church in "tempering the body together," (1 Cor. 12:24, KJV).

Christ is the avowed Head of the Church; therefore, it should be the goal of church leadership to join each member to Christ. "He who is joined to the Lord is one spirit with Him" (1 Cor. 6:17). Sometimes, pastors join church members to themselves rather than to Christ. This unnatural bonding actually seduces the people away from Christ. Such ungodly soul ties may be formed by the intentional designs of the pastor, or they may be initiated by members of the congregation who idolize the pastor above Christ. Cults are often an outgrowth of these kinds of soul ties.

I recall ministering deliverance to a pastor who idolized his spiritual mentor to the extent that he would not listen to any other minister's recorded messages. He prided himself that he had every cassette tape that his idolized teacher had made. This pastor walked with a limp in emulation of his teacher who had a lame leg. When his teacher had a heart attack, this pastor developed chest pains. As we ministered deliverance to this pastor, the demon in him cried out, "I am fellowshipping with him [the idolized minister] in his suffering!" (see Phil. 3:10).

The Apostle Paul countered this same unhealthy soul tie when he said to the church at Corinth:

> For where there are envy, strife, and divisions among you, are you not carnal and behaving like mere men? For when one says, "I am of Paul," and another, "I am of Apollos," are you not carnal? Who then is Paul, and who is Apollos, but ministers through whom you believed.
>
> 1 Cor. 3:3–5

Paul went on to explain that Christ is the only foundation that can be laid. When man replaces Christ as the foundation, the spirit of Antichrist is introduced. This is the sort of error that took place within some elements of the Shepherding movement. The shepherd of the local flock became: the "I Am" to his sheep, so that no action took place except through the human shepherd.

Spiritual leaders must maintain the spirit of John the Baptist who declared, "I am not the Christ... but the *friend* of the bridegroom" (John 3:28–29, EMPHASIS MINE). Otherwise, one usurps the position of Christ as Head of the Church and ties the people to himself. When loyalties are tied to man rather than to Christ, Christian fellowship with other churches and denominations is either hindered or made impossible.

Demons of doctrinal error have been known to identify themselves by the name of the leader who fostered the error. In such cases the demonic soul tie is clearly identified.

Influence of Like Spirits

How do demons enter into soul ties? Evil spirits are able to enter when spiritual boundaries are violated. God has set boundaries that govern our relationships with others. God has given man a nature to love and to live in association with others, but God has set boundaries for all such relationships. For example, there are protective boundaries set by God for marriage. A man is to forsake all others and be joined to his wife. There are similar limitations that govern friendships and bonds within the Body of Christ. When relationships within any given area disregard the boundaries that God has established, the relationships become perverse and demons enter. In other words, fleshly soul ties become demonic soul ties.

Through soul ties, a spiritual channel is formed. For example, in a godly marriage, the Holy Spirit flows between husband and wife so that revelations and workings of the Holy Spirit are held in common between a man and his wife. The two become one through the influence of the Holy Spirit on their lives. The same principle operates in demonic soul ties. When there is a sinful joining of two individuals, demon spirits in one person open up the other person for similar spirits, and the two become one.

the Power of Soul Ties

The power of soul ties is reflected in two important words in the Greek New Testament: "joined" and "fellowship."

"Joined"

The word "joined" is used in relation to marriage. In Ephesians 5:31 we are told that a man is to be "JOINED" unto his wife. The literal meaning in Greek is: to cleave, stick to, glue or cement. Another use of "joined" is found in Matthew 19:6 where we are told concerning marriage: "Therefore what God has joined together, let not man separate." "Joined" can be translated as "yoked together."

Within marriage, one can plumb the heights and depths of human relationship. The soul tie between husband and wife is pure and satisfying. The times of "coming together" can be a ministry to one another under the anointing of the Holy Spirit. If, however; the husband introduces oral or anal sex (sodomy) into the relationship, then another spirit is introduced; and the wife becomes defiled by the transference of the unclean spirit in him to herself.

The word "joined" is also used in relationship to the Church. Ephesians 4:16 speaks of "The whole body, *joined and knit* together" (EMPHASIS MINE). Again, in 1 Cor. 1:10, we read, "Now I plead with you, brethren, by the name of our Lord Jesus Christ, that you all speak the same thing, and that there be no divisions among you; but that ye be *perfectly joined* together in the same mind and in the same judgment" (EMPHASIS MINE).

The Church is one body. "And if one member suffers, all the members suffer with it" (1 Cor. 12:26). That is, whatever happens to one member affects the other members of the Body. "Do you not know that your bodies are the members of Christ? Shall I then take the members of Christ and make them members of a harlot? Certainly not!" (1 Cor. 6:15). Therefore, when a church member engages in sexual immorality, Christ the Head is affected; and each member of the body is affected. This is the reason that there must be church discipline in such matters to remove any unrepentant sinner. For example, the man in the Corinthian church who was living incestuously, was to be excommunicated. Paul explained:

"Do you not know that a little leaven leavens the whole lump? Therefore purge out the old leaven, that you may be a new lump."

1 Cor. 5:6–7

We have known of churches whose members fell into sexual sin in wholesale fashion. A spirit of fornication ruled those churches. Perhaps it was a pastor who first fell into adultery, but it could have been any member of the Body who committed the sin. Since each member is "joined" to the other members; when one sins, the whole body is affected.

Furthermore, the word "joined" describes our relationship with Christ. "But he who is joined to the Lord is one spirit with Him" (1 Cor. 6:17, EMPHASIS MINE). Just as a husband or wife can commit adultery against his/her spouse, a person can commit spiritual adultery against the Lord. Idolatry is spiritual harlotry. Every occult practice is an expression of idolatry, and by participating in anything occult a person goes outside his relationship with God to receive forbidden knowledge, wisdom, guidance or power. The person who has relationship with idols is said to have "joined" himself to that idol.

So Israel was *joined* to Baal of Peor [an idol of Moab], and the anger of the Lord was aroused against Israel.

Num. 25:3.

They *joined* themselves also to Baal of Peor, And ate sacrifices made to the dead.

Ps. 106:28.

Ephraim is *joined* to idols, let him alone.

Hos. 4:17 (EMPHASIS MINE)

When a person goes to a fortune teller, he "joins" himself to that occult practioner by a spiritual connection and, therefore, commits spiritual adultery. By spiritual adultery, a spiritual soul tie is formed. Through occult involvement, one has spiritual intercourse with demons!

"Fellowship"

We have **fellowship** with Christ through His sacrifice on cross.

> The cup of blessing which we bless, is it not the communion of the blood of Christ? The bread which we break, is it not the communion of the body of Christ? For we, being many, are one bread and one body: for we all partake of that one bread.
>
> 1 Cor. 10:16, 17

The Greek word "fellowship" means communion, partaking together, sharing in common. As Christians, our communion is in Christ. We become "one body" by partaking together of the One Bread which is Christ who is broken for us. When we sit at the Lord's table and partake of the bread and wine of communion, we are partaking of His sacrifice. This is fellowship based on our sharing in His sacrificial death for the atonement of our sins.

We have "fellowship" with demons through idolatry. What happens when we participate in an idolatrous activity such as hypnotism, the Ouija Board, astrology or divination? We have sat at another table: the table of idols.

> Therefore, my beloved, flee from idolatry... You cannot drink the cup of the Lord and the cup of demons; you cannot partake of the Lord's table and of the table of demons.
>
> 1 Cor. 10:14, 21

How does the Lord feel about our fellowship with demons? "We provoke the Lord to jealousy" (1 Cor. 10:22). If a wife goes out with another man, the husband is jealous. Likewise, a Christian's affair with "another spirit" provokes the Lord to jealousy. Soul ties made through occult involvement must be renounced and destroyed.

Husbands and wives who truly become "one flesh" will think alike, act alike and may even look alike. God's Word says that when people are joined to idols they become like their idols:

> Their idols are silver and gold, The work of men's hands. They have mouths, but they do not speak; Eyes they have, but they do not see; They have ears, but they do not hear; Noses they have, but they do not smell; They have hands, but they do not handle; feet they have, but they do not walk; Nor do they mutter through their throat. *Those who make them are like them; so is everyone who trusts in them.*
> Ps. 115:4–8 (EMPHASIS MINE)

BREAKING DEMONIC SOUL TIES

Through our study we have come to see that demonic soul ties are indeed prevalent and more far-reaching than we may have supposed. As evil soul ties are identified, what can be done to reverse their power?

First, repentance toward God is necessary. God's ordinances have been violated. Lust has taken us beyond the boundaries of purity that the Lord set for us. Even if the sin was committed ignorance, it still requires forgiveness. Ask God NOW to forgive you for each perverse soul tie that you have created.

Second, spoil the devil's house by taking back all that he has gained against you. Confess before God that Satan has no further legal right to you. Declare that each demonic soul tie that you have identified is now destroyed in the name of the Lord Jesus Christ.

Third, command the evil spirits associated with the soul ties to leave you in the Name of Jesus Christ, the Son of God.

Note: Be as specific as possible when breaking soul ties. Soul ties are formed with each person with whom one has had sexual relationships outside of marriage. Name each sexual partner by name and verbally renounce the ties with each one. Are there soul ties with animals? Are there any wrong ties with family members? Are there abnormal ties with pastors or people within the Body of Christ? Have spiritually perverse soul ties been created through association with occultists such as: diviners, astrologers, witches, charmers, mediums, necromancers, hypnotists, ear piercers (Exod. 21:5, 6), tattoo artists (Lev. 19:28), blood covenanters, or unholy vows with Free Masons, fraternity brothers or sorority sisters?

Ask for and accept God's forgiveness for each evil soul that you ever formed. In the name of Jesus, command all demons associated with perverse soul ties to go.

TO SEE A SHORT VIDEO OF FRANK HAMMOND TEACHING ON THE REALITY OF *SOUL TIES*, AND HOW TO BREAK THEM, VISIT THE FOLLOWING WEBSITE:

www.impactchristianbooks.com/soulties

Books, Booklets & Audio – Video

by Frank & Ida Mae Hammond

Books

The Breaking of Curses

Comfort for the Wounded Spirit

Demons & Deliverance: In the Ministry of Jesus

A Manual for Children's Deliverance

Kingdom Living for the Family

Overcoming Rejection

Pigs in the Parlor

Study Guide: Pigs in the Parlor

Saints at War - Warfare in the Heavenlies

Booklets

Confronting Familiar Spirits

Soul Ties

Repercussions from Sexual Sins

The Marriage Bed

Forgiving Others

Our Warfare

The Father's Blessing

God Warns America

The Perils of Passivity

Promoted by God

The Strongman of Unbelief

The Tales of Two Franks

Obstacles to Deliverance / Why Deliverance Sometimes Fails

DVD Videos

The Schizophrenia Revelation

Breaking Demonic Soul Ties

Breaking Curses

The Wiles of the Devil

Obstacles to Deliverance

Binding the Strongman

The Mind, Will & Emotions

Deliverance from Self

Can a Christian Have a Demon?

Compact Discs

The Deliverance Series (6 CDs)

The End-Time Series (6 CDs)

Faith Series (6 CDs)

Spiritual Meat Series (6 CDs)

Message on Love (5 CDs)

Freedom from Bondage (6 CDs)

Family in the Kingdom (6 CDs)

Walk in the Spirit Series (6 CDs)

The Church Series (6 CDs)

Recognizing God (3 CDs)

Available at **www.impactchristianbooks.com**

Do Your Relationships Produce
Bondage or Joy?

Does someone manipulate you?

What are the symptoms of an ungodly relationship?

Are you tormented with thoughts of a former lover or friend?

Are you free to be all that God intended you to be?

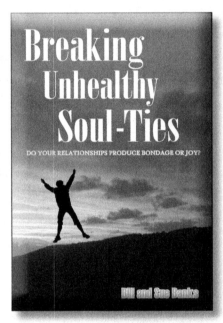

9780892281398

Study Guide - 9780892282043

"Here at last is a thorough and theologically sound treatment of a little understood subject" - from the *Foreword* by Frank Hammond

Breaking Unhealthy Soul-Ties
by Bill & Sue Banks

Unhealthy soul-ties involve the control of one individual over another, and can be one of the most difficult blocks to spiritual freedom. Some relationships are healthy and bring blessings into our lives; other types of relationships can bring demonic bondage to our souls. This book assists the reader in diagnosing both healthy and unhealthy relationships, and offers positive steps to personal freedom.

FRANK HAMMOND BOOKS

PIGS IN THE PARLOR* 0892280271

A handbook for deliverance from demons and spiritual oppression, patterned after the ministry of Jesus Christ. With over 1 million copies in print worldwide, and translated into more than a dozen languages, *Pigs in the Parlor* remains the authoritative book on the subject of deliverance.

STUDY GUIDE: PIGS IN THE PARLOR 0892281995

Designed as a study tool for either individuals or groups, this guide will enable you to diagnose your personal deliverance needs, walk you through the process of becoming free, and equip you to set others free from demonic torment. Includes questions and answers on a chapter-by-chapter basis as well as new information to further your knowledge of deliverance.

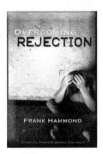

OVERCOMING REJECTION* 0892281057

Frank Hammond addresses the all-too-common root problem of rejection and the fear of rejection in the lives of believers, and provides steps to be set free. Learn how past experiences can influence our actions, and how we can be made whole.

THE BREAKING OF CURSES* 089228109x

The Bible refers to curses more than 230 times, and 70 sins that cause curses are put forth in Scripture. Learn how Curses are just as real today as in Biblical times. This book shows what curses are and how you may deliver yourself and your family from them.

A MANUAL FOR CHILDREN'S DELIVERANCE 0892280786

The Hammonds' book for ministering to children is a valuable tool for parents to learn how to set their children free from spiritual bondages. Learn the basics of how to effectively minister deliverance to children.

* Also available in Spanish

OTHER FRANK HAMMOND BOOKS & E-BOOKS

CONFRONTING FAMILIAR SPIRITS 0892280174

A person can form and develop a close relationship with an evil spirit, willfully or through ignorance, for knowledge or gain. When a person forms a relationship with an evil spirit, he then has a familiar spirit. Familiar spirits are counterfeits of the Holy Spirit's work.

REPERCUSSIONS FROM SEXUAL SINS 0892282053

The sexual revolution has impacted our nation, our church and our family. Promiscuity, nudity and sexual obscenities have become commonplace. The inevitable consequence of defilement is the loss of fellowship with a holy God. Learn how to break free from the bondage of sexual sin.

THE MARRIAGE BED 0892281863

Can the marriage bed be defiled? Or, does anything and everything go so long as husband and wife are in agreement with their sexual activities? Drawing from God's emphasis on purity and holiness in our lives, this booklet explains how to avoid perverse sexual demonic activity in a home.

FORGIVING OTHERS 089228076X

Unforgiveness brings a curse, and can be a major roadblock to the deliverance and freedom of your soul. Find the spiritual truths regarding the necessity of forgiveness and the blessings of inner freedom which result!

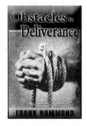

OBSTACLES TO DELIVERANCE 0892282037

Why does deliverance sometimes fail? This is, in essence, the same question raised by Jesus' first disciples, when they were unable to cast out a spirit of epilepsy. Jesus gave a multi-part answer which leads us to take into account the strength of the spirit confronted and the strategy of warfare employed.

THE PERILS OF PASSIVITY 089228160X

Some have made deliverance their ultimate goal in life. Deliverance is not a final goal, it is only a sub-goal on the way to fulfill God's purpose in life. God said to Pharaoh, "Let my people go that they may serve Me..." (Exod. 7:16). There is a purpose in God for each of us - and it is not passivity! Passivity is a foe — it will even block deliverance.

Lightning Source UK Ltd.
Milton Keynes UK
UKOW04f1800050716

277761UK00027B/551/P